ZORA HURSTON *and the* CHINABERRY TREE

ZORA HURSTON and the CHINABERRY TREE

written by WILLIAM MILLER

Illustrated by CORNELIUS VAN WRIGHT *and* YING-HWA HU

LEE & LOW BOOKS Inc.   *New York*

Text copyright © 1994 by William Miller
Illustrations copyright © 1994 by Cornelius Van Wright and Ying-Hwa Hu
All rights reserved. No part of the contents of this book may be reproduced
by any means without the written permission of the publisher.
LEE & LOW BOOKS Inc., 95 Madison Avenue, New York, NY 10016

Printed in Hong Kong by South China Printing Co. (1988) Ltd.

Book Design by Christy Hale
Book Production by Our House

The text is set in Bell.
The illustrations are rendered in watercolors on paper.

10 9 8 7 6 5 4 3
First Edition

Library of Congress Cataloging-in-Publication Data
Miller, William,
Zora Hurston and the chinaberry tree/by William Miller;
illustrated by Cornelius Van Wright and Ying-Hwa Hu.—1st ed.
p. cm.
ISBN 1-880000-33-4 (paperback)
1. Hurston, Zora Neale—Biography—Juvenile literature.
2. Afro-American women authors—20th century—Biography—Juvenile literature.
[1. Hurston, Zora Neale. 2. Authors, American.
3. Afro-Americans—Biography. 4. Women—Biography.]
I. Van Wright, Cornelius, ill. II. Hu, Ying-Hwa, ill. III. Title.
PS3515.U789Z786 1994
813'.52—dc20   94-1291
[B] CIP AC

For Charles Ghigna, teacher and friend
                                    —W.M.

In memory of our sister Linda,
May her children always jump at the sun
                                    —C.V.W. & Y.H.

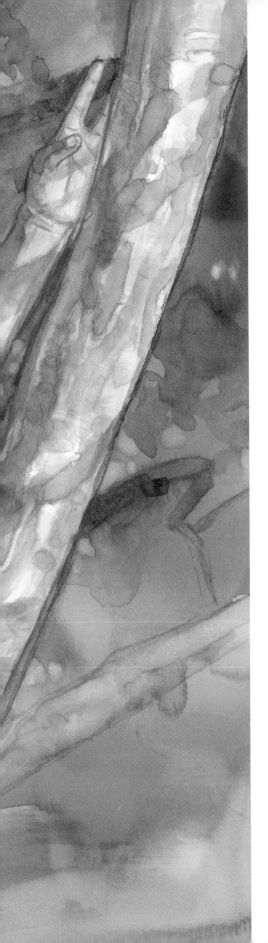

Zora Hurston loved the chinaberry tree.

Her mother taught her to climb it, one branch at a time.

From the tree, she could see as far
as the lake, as far as the horizon.

Zora dreamed of fishing in the lake,
catching bream and catfish in the moonlight.

Zora dreamed of seeing the cities beyond
the horizon, of living there one day.

But only boys fished in the lake,
only men traveled to the cities.

Zora watched with envy as the wagons
rattled down the dusty roads.

Her father told her to wear a dress,
to leave tree-climbing to wild boys
who had no better way to spend their time.

He told her to read the Bible every day,
learn verses she could recite in Sunday school.

He warned her about girls who didn't obey
their fathers, girls who didn't grow up to be
young ladies.

But Zora only listened to her mother.

She taught Zora that everything had a voice:
the trees and rushing wind, the stars
in the midnight sky.

She taught Zora that the world belonged
to her, even the lake and far-off horizon.

So Zora went everywhere.

She walked into the town store and watched while the men played checkers.

She asked questions and more questions until the men taught her how to play.

She followed boys to the edge of campfires,
listened while their fathers sang about John Henry:

a man so strong he swung a nine-pound
hammer from dawn till dusk.

She learned about Death, the great square-toed
one who lived in the west.

Death sat on a platform made of palm leaves
and ruled with a sword in his hands.

Zora learned about Africa, the place where
she and her people came from.

In Africa they had been kings and queens,
builders of cities that stood for thousands of years.

They worshipped Gods who ruled the sky,
the mountains and rivers, the stormy sea . . . .

One morning Zora's mother didn't feel well.

She told Zora not to worry, that soon she would be well again. She told Zora to go outside and play, to climb her favorite tree.

But Zora couldn't play. She saw how tired her mother was. She saw the pain in her eyes.

Day after day, Zora sat beside her mother's bed telling her the stories she had heard beside the campfires.

Her mother smiled and asked Zora to always remember what she had learned.

Stories, she said, kept their people alive. As long as they were told, Africa would live in their hearts.

Zora promised to remember.

Zora's mother slowly got worse.
Men and women came to sit up with her
through the long, hot nights.

The town doctor came. He gave her pills
and shook his head, walked sadly away.

Even the root doctor tried his magic.
He rubbed snake oil and mustard salve
on her face; he burned a tall white candle
beside her bed.

But nothing worked.

Zora was sitting in the parlor when her
father told her she would not see her
mother again.

Zora felt as if she had died. She watched while the old people stopped the clocks, put sheets on the mirr

She watched while the women cried and the m stared at their Sunday shoes.

But then she could sit still no mo.

Zora ran from the house, ran all the way
to the chinaberry tree.

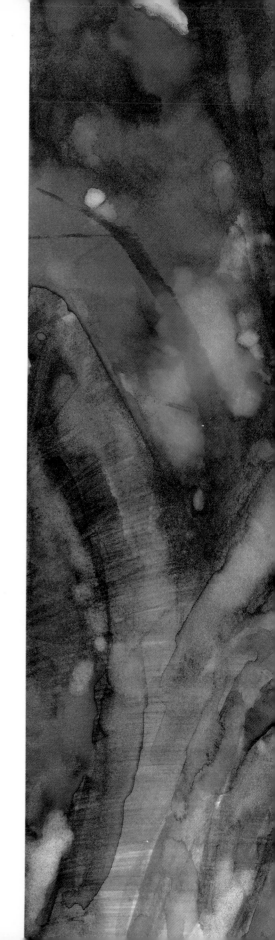

She climbed the first branch and the next,
climbed almost to the top.

A sparrow sang to her in a voice like her
mother's. The sparrow told her
not to give up, to climb even higher.

From the top of the tree Zora saw again
the world her mother had given her:

the lake filled with fish, the cities where she would
tell people all she had learned beside the campfires.

Zora promised her mother that she would
never stop climbing,

would always reach for the newborn sky,

always jump at the morning sun!

AUTHOR'S NOTE

Zora Hurston was born in 1891. She grew up in Eatonville, Florida, the first all-black, incorporated town in America. At an early age, she was exposed to the rich oral tradition of her community: stories, songs, and folktales that celebrated African American life.

Zora attended Howard University and Barnard College, where she studied anthropology. She traveled throughout the South recording the folktales of her people. She published these stories in a collection called *Mules and Men*. Zora was also the author of many works of fiction. Her most famous novel, *Their Eyes Were Watching God,* is a classic of African American literature.